Dawn Price

... are
...ountries
...hilst
... flood?

Acknowledgements

Mark Boulton/Alamy: 27 (bottom); Ron Buskirk/Alamy: 13 (left); Chad Ehlers/Alamy: 15 (left); m c photography/Alamy: 16 (top); Jenny Matthews/Alamy: 21 (top); Ace Stock Limited/Alamy: 25 (top); Charlotte Thege/Alamy: 26 (top); Realimage/Alamy: 27 (top); The Photolibrary Wales/Alamy: 25 (bottom); Mark Sykes/Alamy: 16 (bottom); Paul Glendell/Alamy: 13 (right); ©Andrew Brown; Ecoscene/Corbis: 8; ©Kyle Niemi/U.S. Coast Guard/ZUMA/Corbis: 19; ©Jim Winkley; Ecoscene/Corbis : 20 (top); ©spotlight-studios - Fotolia.com: 4 (top); ©Oleg Ivanov - Fotolia.com: 4 (centre); ©Peter Galbraith - Fotolia.com: 4 (bottom); Daniel Berehulak/Getty Images: 17 (top); Robert Cianflone/Getty Images: 21 (left), 22 (right); Francoise De Mulder/Roger Viollet/Getty Images: 23 (left); Chris Jackson/Getty Images: 20 (bottom); Adi Shah/AFP/Getty Images: 18; David Silverman/Getty Images: 17 (bottom); Edmond Terakopian/AFP/Getty Images: 15 (right); Amir Shah/AP/PA Photos: 23 (right); Lewis Whyld/PA Archive/PA Photos: 14; ©Stuart Freedman/Panos: 26 (bottom); ©Dieter Telemans/Panos: 21 (bottom); WaterAid: 28 (top); WaterAid/Caroline Irby: 29; WaterAid/Caroline Penn: 28

United Kingdom: Folens Publishers, Waterslade House, Thame Road, Haddenham, Buckinghamshire HP17 8NT.
www.folens.com

Ireland: Folens Publishers, Greenhills Road, Tallaght, Dublin 24.
Email: info@folens.ie

Editor: Mairi Sutherland
Series designer: Fiona Webb
Illustrations: Celia Hart and Tony Randell
Cover design: Design by Form (www.form.uk.com)
Back cover photos: m c photography/Alamy (top right); Chris Jackson/Getty images (bottom left); WaterAid/Caroline Irby (bottom right)
Picture researcher: Sophie Hartley

Every effort has been made to trace the copyright holders of material used in this publication. If any copyright holder has been overlooked, we should be pleased to make any necessary arrangements.

British Library Cataloguing in Publication Data. A catalogue record for this publication is available from the British Library.

ISBN 978 1 85008 310 8

Contents

Why does the rain never stop?

Have you ever thought about how water gets to the tap? Or why there is so much water in the oceans? And why sometimes the rain keeps falling and falling? In this lesson we will find out what the water cycle is, how it works and how humans can affect it.

a Water as a liquid

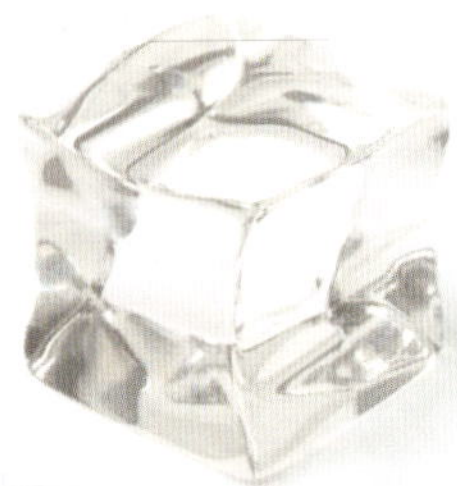

b Water as solid ice

c Water as a gas

What is water like?

Before we think about how water moves, we need to think about what it is actually like. A water molecule is made up of oxygen and hydrogen. Its chemical formula is written like this: H_2O. Water exists in three states:

- **liquid water** (rivers, streams and oceans)
- **solid ice** (glaciers, snow and ice cubes)
- **gas or water vapour** (steam from a kettle).

What is the water cycle?

The amount of water in the world always stays the same. It just changes its state as it moves through the water cycle. There are four main processes in the watercycle: **evaporation**, **transpiration**, **condensation** and **precipitation**.

CHALLENGE

1 a) Look at pictures a–c. What is the link between them? Which is the odd one out, and why?
   b) What percentage of the world's water do you think is in each of these states?

2 a) The following changes in state are involved in the different processes of the water cycle:
   - liquid to gas
   - gas to liquid
   - liquid to gas via a plant

   Which change goes with which process? Use diagram d to help you.
   b) If precipitation is the only process that does not involve a change of state, what do you think it does involve and how could we define it?

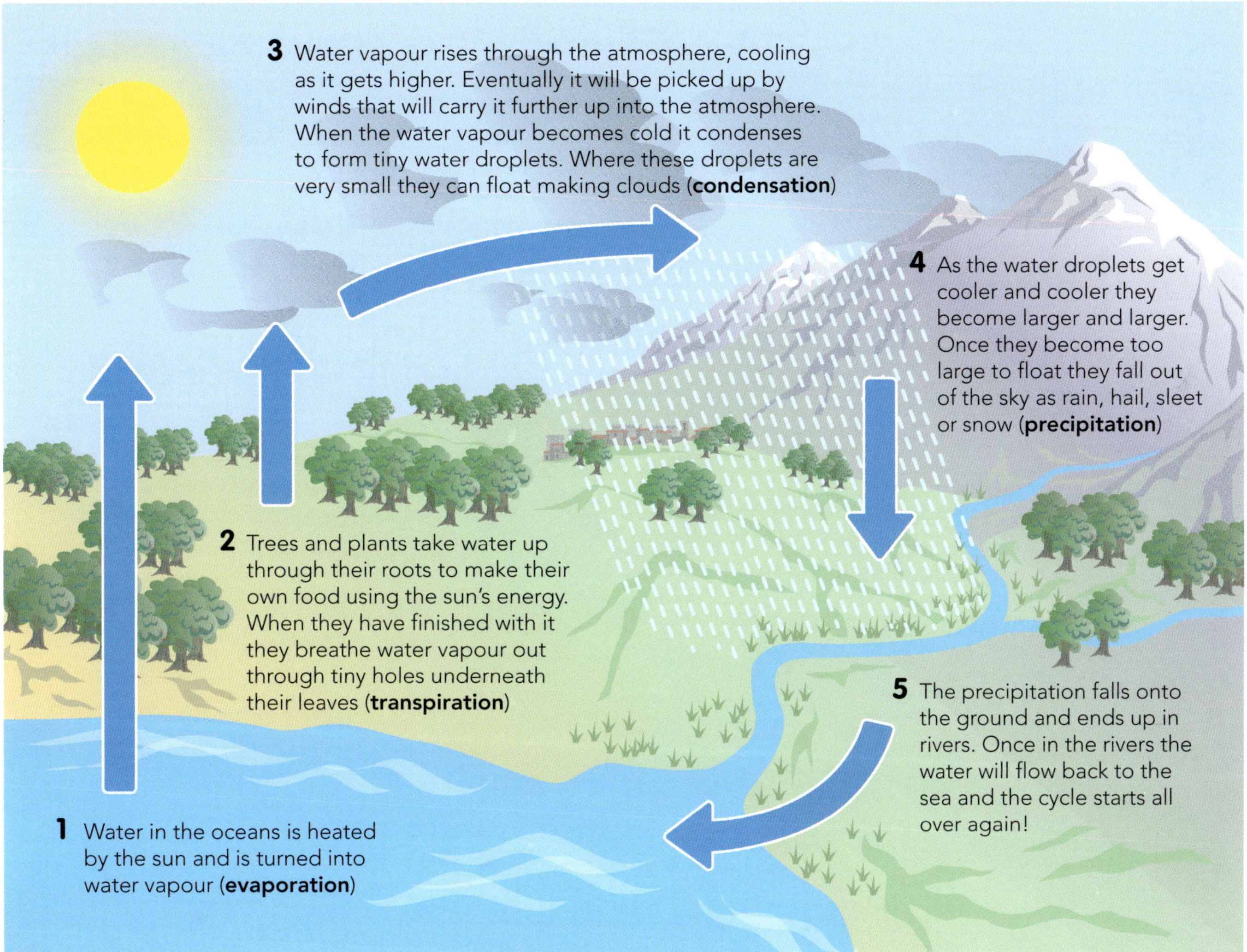

d The water cycle

CHALLENGE

3 Draw a simple diagram of the water cycle. Add the following labels to your diagram, and number them to show the order in which the processes happen.

- Rivers flow to the seas and oceans.
- Plants and trees breathe out water vapour through tiny holes in their leaves. This process is called transpiration.
- Warm air rises, then cools to form tiny water droplets that make clouds. This process is called condensation.
- The sun heats up the lakes and oceans, turning liquid water to water vapour. This process is called evaporation.
- The water droplets get bigger and bigger until they get too heavy and fall from the sky as precipitation.
- When precipitation hits the ground it can soak in or move across the surface, ending up in rivers.

4 Imagine that you are a water droplet. Look at all the information on pages 4 and 5 and draw a flow chart to show the different things that could happen to you in a day. You could think about what will happen to you if you travel to different places: water droplets in the Arctic will do different things to water drops in India!

Where does a river start and where does it go?

The water cycle showed us that water moves continuously around a system. We will now find out how precipitation gets into a river and how a river changes as the water in it flows towards the sea.

How does precipitation get into rivers?

When water hits the ground it can move in three different ways: over, through or under. Whichever way it goes, because of gravity, it moves downhill until it ends up in a river. Rivers are always at the bottom of a valley.

You can see this by pouring water onto a dry sponge on a plastic surface. Some of the water reaches the plastic surface quickly (the water moves underground). Some of the water is soaked up by the sponge and travels through it (the water moves through the ground). And, once the sponge is full the water moves across the surface of the sponge (the water moves over ground).

The diagram below shows the three ways water – or precipitation – flows into a river.

CHALLENGE

1 Look at diagram a.
   a) When it hits the ground, precipitation flows in three ways to reach a river. Which flow is the quickest and why? Which flow is the slowest and why?
   b) Do you think the water table stays in the same place all the time? Why?

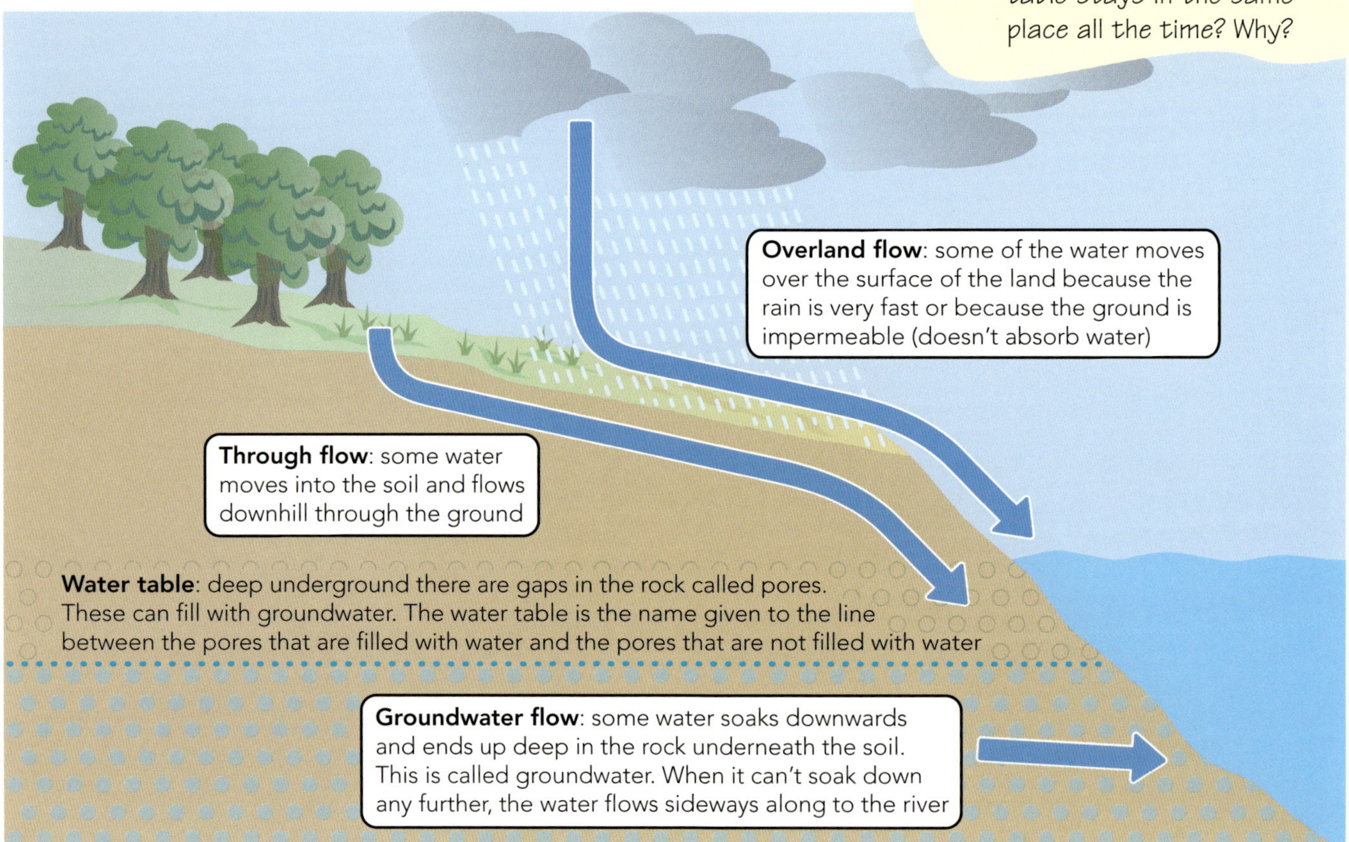

a The three different ways water flows into a river

What happens to the water in a river?

Every river flows through a **drainage basin**. A drainage basin is like a giant sink: any water that falls into it drains out through the 'plug hole', the river. Diagram b shows the features of a river on its journey from its source to the sea. Every river – large or small, long or short – has these features.

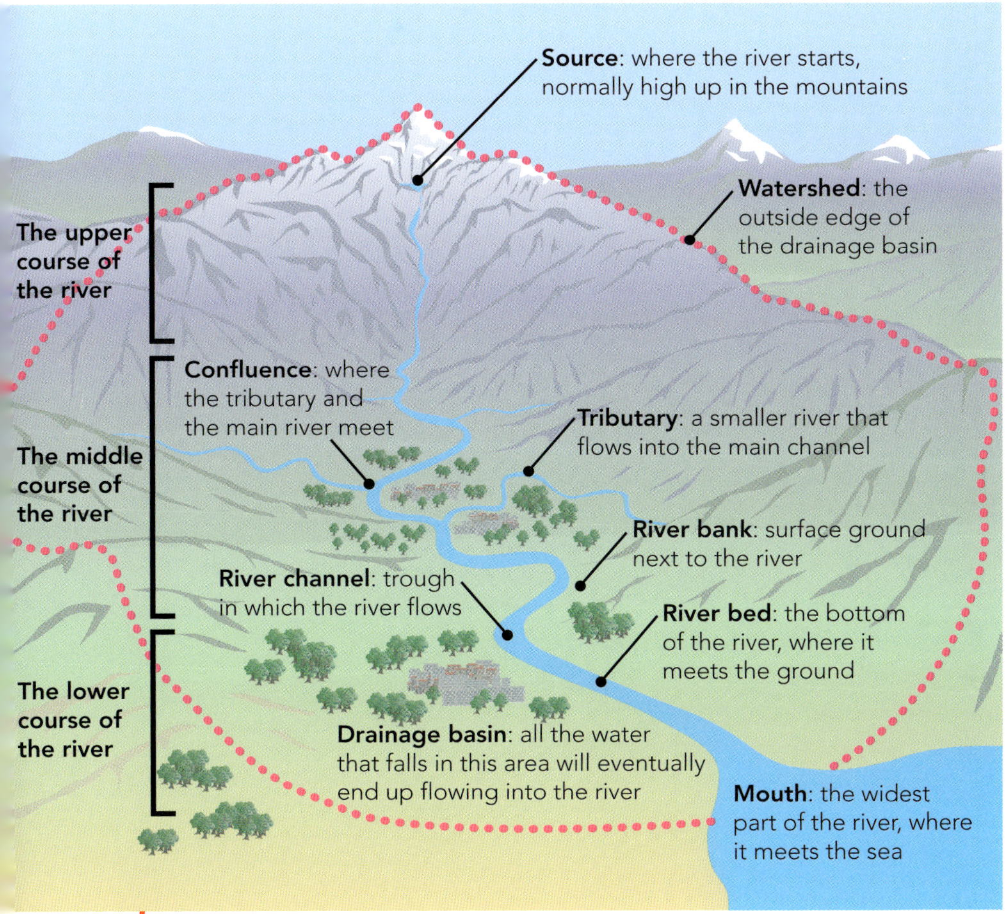

b Drainage basin, which shows a river's journey from source to sea

What is the long profile?

If you imagine that a river is straight and you cut it in half from the source to the mouth you get the **long profile**. It shows the height of the land along the length of the river. In the upper course the slope is steep; in the middle course the slope is gentle; in the lower course the slope flattens out at the river mouth.

CHALLENGE

2 Use diagram b to help you to answer these clues:
   a) The line around a drainage basin (9)
   b) It's a bit like a sink! (8, 5)
   c) The point where two rivers meet (10)
   d) The river doesn't sleep here! (5, 3)
   e) Where the river flows (5, 7)
   f) Where the river starts (6)

3 Draw a diagram to show the long profile of a river and label the upper course, the middle course and the lower course.

4 The River Severn is Britain's longest river. Find a map of the River Severn in an atlas or on Google Earth. Now see if you can find out the following:
   a) Where is the source of the River Severn and how high is it?
   b) Where is the mouth of the River Severn and what is it called?
   c) What are the names of six towns along the river?
   d) What are the names of six major tributaries?
   e) How long is the River Severn?
   HINT: Think back to your lessons on map skills.

What happens in a river?

We have seen how a river moves from its source to the sea. In this lesson we are going to learn about the processes that happen in a river, and how the amount of energy in the water influences them.

Where is the energy in a river?

Have you ever tried to stand up in a fast-moving stream or held your hand under a waterfall? It's difficult to keep still, isn't it? This is because of the force of the moving water.

All moving things, including water, have energy. The faster the water is moving, the more energy it has. People sometimes use this energy for their own purposes, and so does nature.

a Moving water has energy!

CHALLENGE

1 a) How many examples can you think of where people have made use of the energy in water?
b) What examples can you think of in nature where the energy in water has caused damage to people, buildings, roads, and so on?
c) How important do you think harnessing the power of water will be in the future to provide us with energy? Why?
d) Do you think that water power will be more important than wind power or solar energy? Why?

What happens when water has lots of energy?

Fast-moving water can be seen in waterfalls, mountain streams, flood waters and in turbulence around obstructions in the river. In these places you can see evidence of the river banks and river bed being worn away. This is called **erosion** and it happens in four ways: abrasion, attrition, hydraulic action and solution.

CHALLENGE

2 Which process of erosion will:

a) be best for making rocks smoother?

b) be best at making banks weaker?

c) have the biggest effect in an area where the river banks are made of soluble rock?

d) help to increase the surface area of the load?

Remember to explain your answers fully!

Erosion

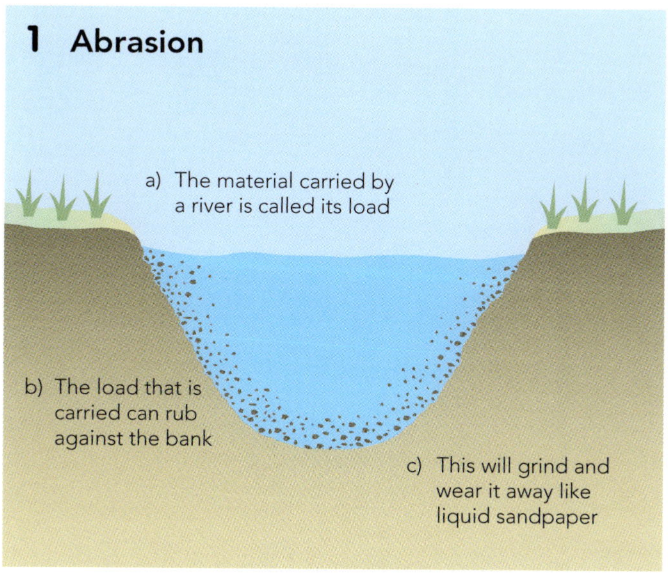

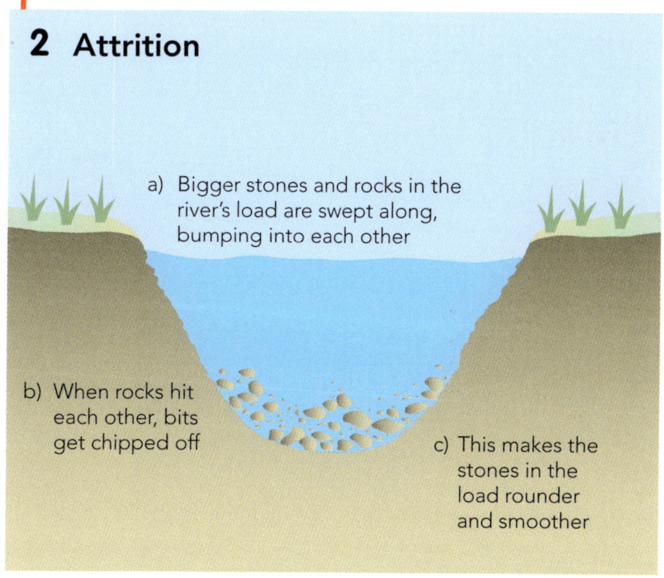

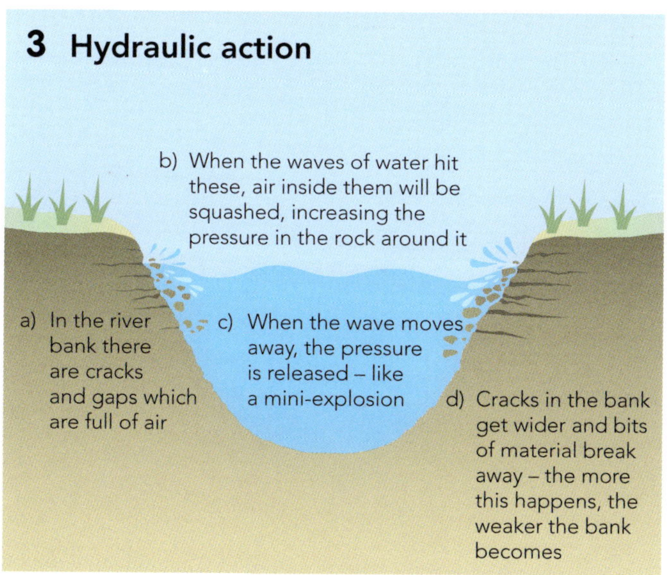

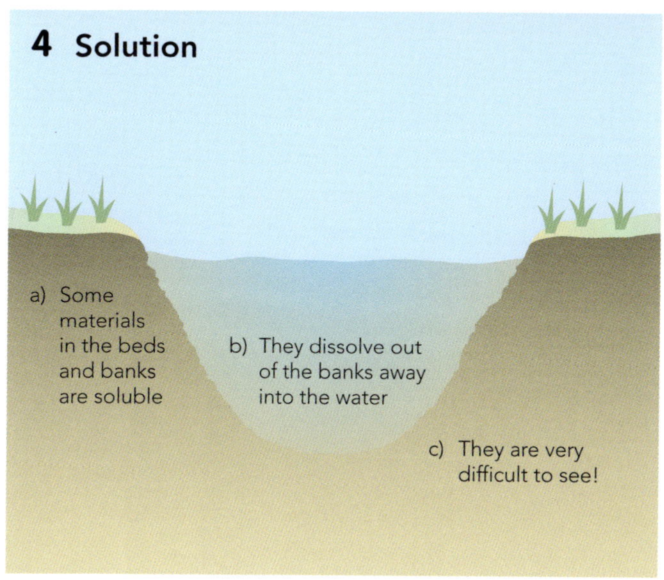

CHALLENGE

3 Which method of transportation will:
   a) move the load furthest?
   b) use the most energy?

What happens when water has a medium amount of energy?

Just like us, rivers cannot be very energetic all the time. Even a bustling mountain stream doesn't have the same energy as a waterfall. When the water has a medium amount of energy it doesn't cause erosion but the energy is still strong enough to keep stones and particles moving along in the water. This process is called **transportation** and again there are four ways in which it happens: traction, saltation, suspension and solution.

Transportation

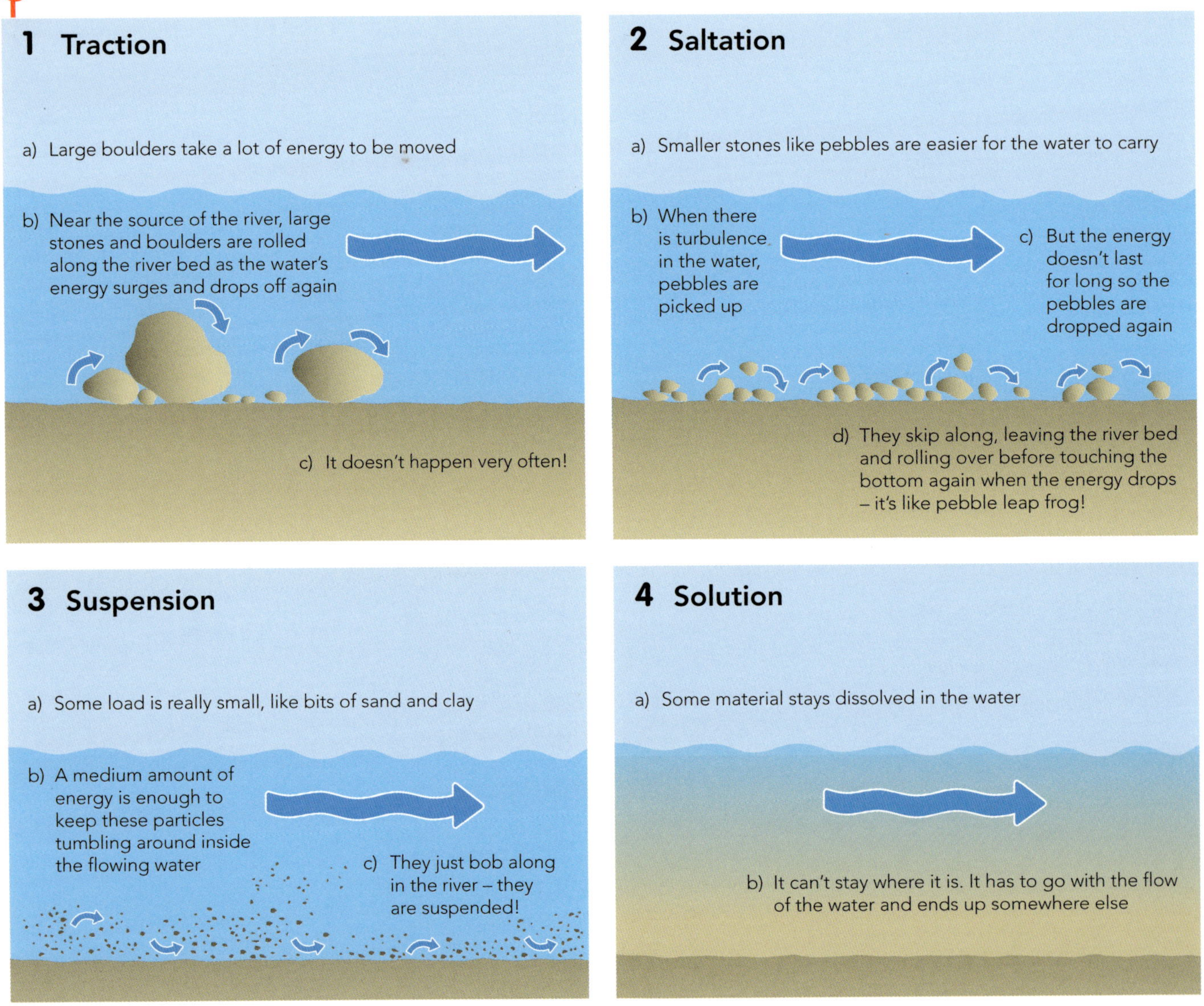

What happens when water only has a little energy?

Even in faster sections of the river there are places where the water slows down: after obstructions or steep drops, or on the inside of a bend. At these points, and especially in the lower course near the sea, water has less energy. It has trouble creating any erosion, except in the very softest soils, and even transportation becomes a bit of a chore. All the bits of the river bed that have been swept along in transportation start falling to the bottom in a process called **deposition**.

Deposition

CHALLENGE

4 Imagine that you have a bottle half-filled with water, you add some soil and some gravel, put the lid on and shake it up. Then put the bottle on the table. What do you think will happen next? In what order will the materials drop to the bottom? Remember to use as many geographical terms to explain your answers as you can.

5 Think back to the long profile of a river. Where is it most likely that erosion, transportation and deposition will take place?

What does a river do to the landscape?

Three processes take place in all rivers: erosion, transportation and deposition. Depending on how much of each process happens, different landforms are formed. And, because the water in a river is always moving, the landforms constantly change.

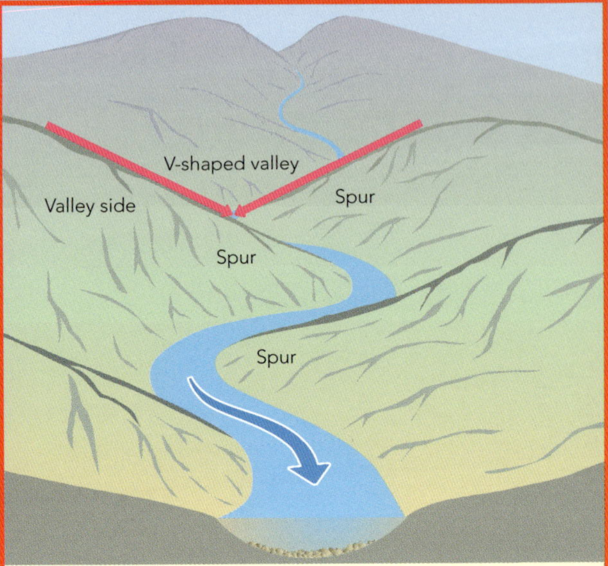

The upper course

In the upper course of the river, although there is a lot of energy, there is not a lot of water. This means there is not enough power for the river to expand sideways, so it cuts downwards. As it keeps cutting downwards over time, a V-shaped valley is created. The water also does not have enough power to cut through obstacles such as hills, so it ends up flowing around them, leaving a spur of land that juts out from the valley side. Over time, interlocking spurs are formed as the river zig-zags from side to side around the spurs.

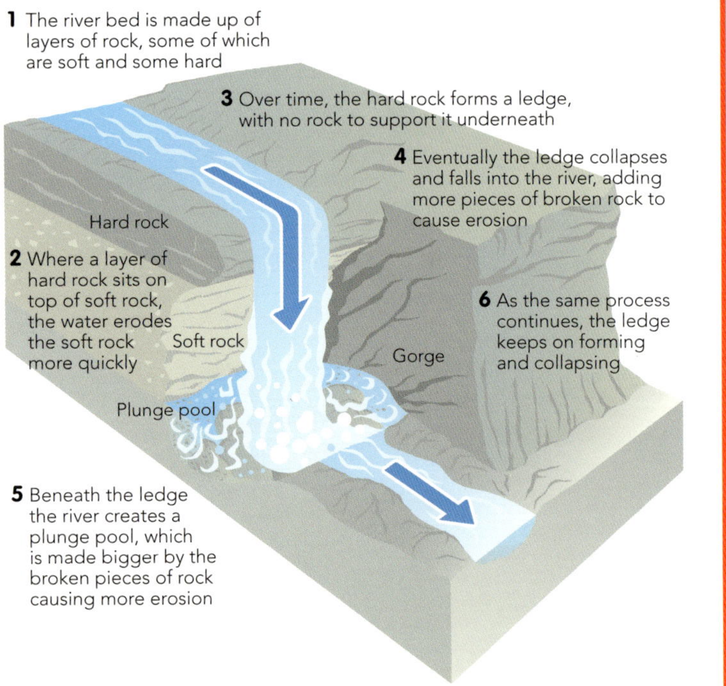

Upper/middle course

Waterfalls often form in the upper/middle course of a river.

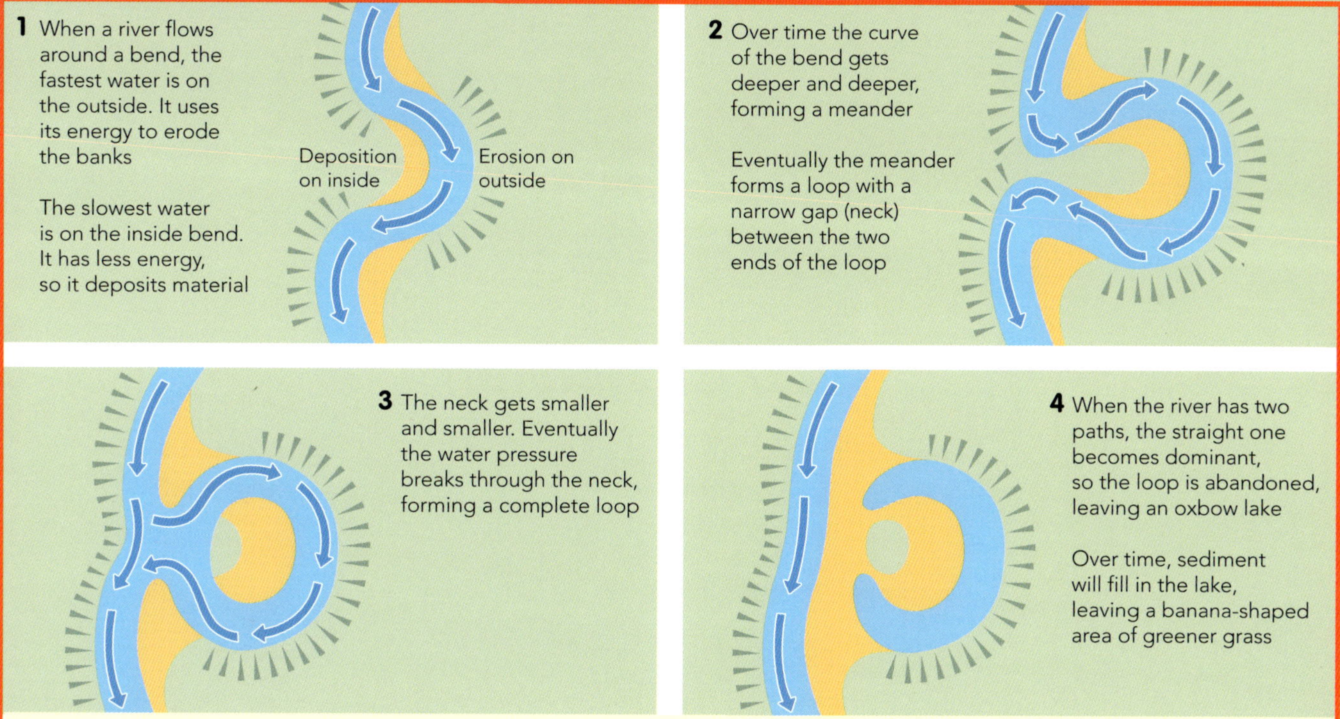

1 When a river flows around a bend, the fastest water is on the outside. It uses its energy to erode the banks

The slowest water is on the inside bend. It has less energy, so it deposits material

2 Over time the curve of the bend gets deeper and deeper, forming a meander

Eventually the meander forms a loop with a narrow gap (neck) between the two ends of the loop

3 The neck gets smaller and smaller. Eventually the water pressure breaks through the neck, forming a complete loop

4 When the river has two paths, the straight one becomes dominant, so the loop is abandoned, leaving an oxbow lake

Over time, sediment will fill in the lake, leaving a banana-shaped area of greener grass

The middle/lower course
In the middle course, the land is a bit flatter and the river forms meanders and oxbow lakes.

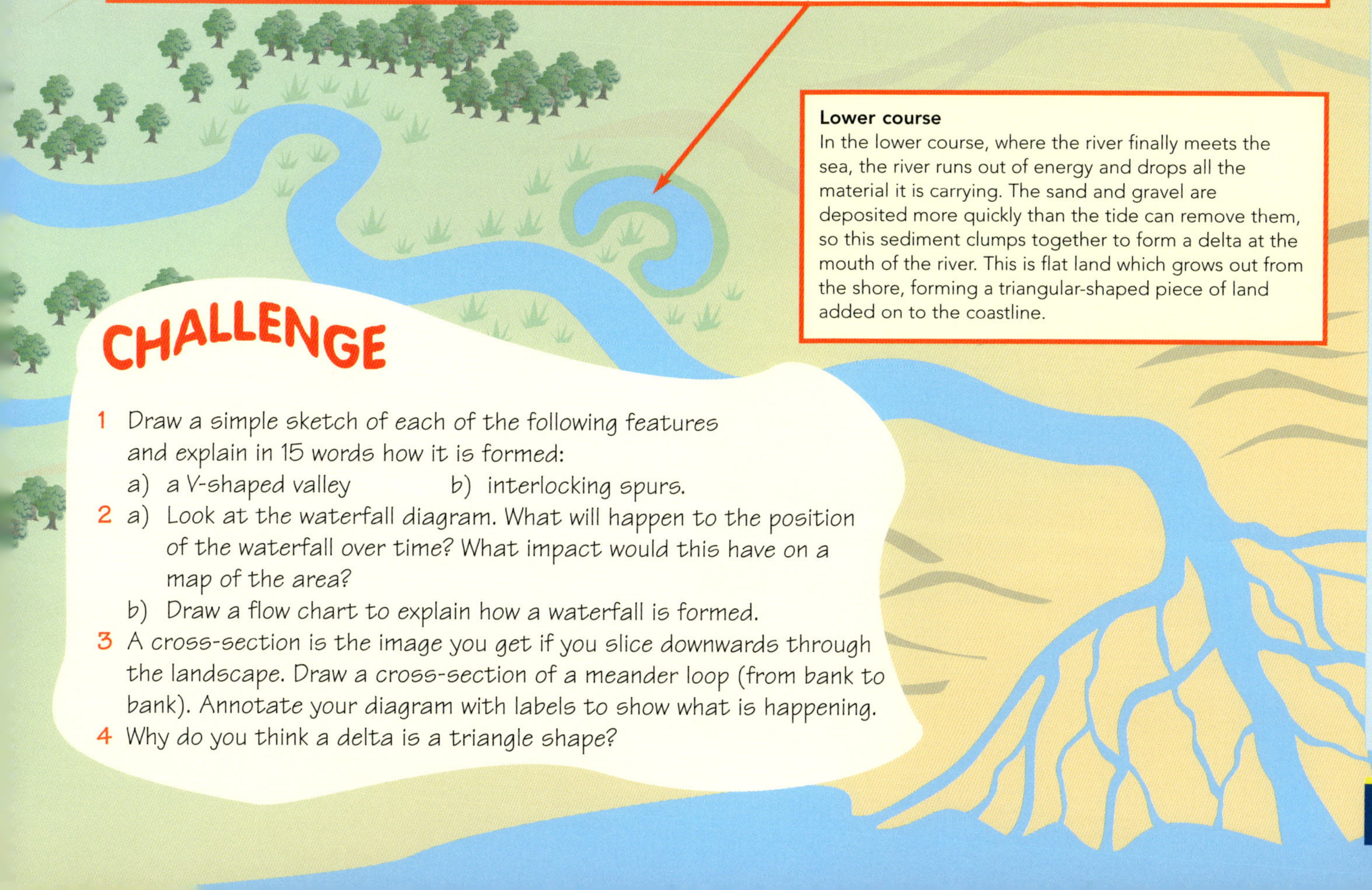

Lower course
In the lower course, where the river finally meets the sea, the river runs out of energy and drops all the material it is carrying. The sand and gravel are deposited more quickly than the tide can remove them, so this sediment clumps together to form a delta at the mouth of the river. This is flat land which grows out from the shore, forming a triangular-shaped piece of land added on to the coastline.

CHALLENGE

1 Draw a simple sketch of each of the following features and explain in 15 words how it is formed:
a) a V-shaped valley b) interlocking spurs.

2 a) Look at the waterfall diagram. What will happen to the position of the waterfall over time? What impact would this have on a map of the area?
b) Draw a flow chart to explain how a waterfall is formed.

3 A cross-section is the image you get if you slice downwards through the landscape. Draw a cross-section of a meander loop (from bank to bank). Annotate your diagram with labels to show what is happening.

4 Why do you think a delta is a triangle shape?

What is a flood?

In June and July 2007, the UK saw some of the worst flooding in living memory. In this lesson we will explore some of the reasons why this extreme weather happened and what the human impacts were.

What is flooding?

Flooding and droughts are part of a natural system, the water cycle. We only view them as hazards because of the effects they have on people. When we understand why floods and droughts occur, we will be better geographers who are more able to predict which areas are more at risk.

Rivers are natural routes for water flowing across land. Provided that the amount of water entering a river system roughly matches the system's ability to get rid of it at the other end, everything will be fine. Flooding is what happens when too much water enters the system or something stops it from following its natural course.

a Dam failure in 2007: firemen pumping water out of Ulley Dam, which is at breaking point, to relieve pressure

What might cause too much water to enter the system?

1 **Heavy rainfall** Large amounts of rain in short periods of time make it difficult for the water to be absorbed into the ground quickly enough. It therefore moves downhill above ground, as surface run-off.
2 **Rapid snow-melt** When temperatures are cold enough, precipitation falls as snow. While temperatures are low, the snow stays above ground. When the temperature rises, the snow melts and large amounts of water are released.
3 **Dam failure** Dams are man-made structures used to hold back the flow of a river. If a dam breaks, a small leak can rapidly become a major collapse and all the water is released in one big surge.

What might stop the water following its natural course?

4 **Saturated ground** Where land is already waterlogged, as it might be after long periods of sustained rain, it won't be able to absorb any more water.

5 **Deforestation** Trees slow water down. They use some of it to help them grow. They also catch some of it as it lands and hold it up as it flows downhill. Deforestation – cutting down large areas of trees – stops this. Water hits the ground harder, moves more quickly and can wash away soil.

6 **Urbanization** Built-up areas are very different to rural areas. They have many more impermeable surfaces (surfaces that don't absorb any water). Drains, rather than natural processes, are responsible for taking water away. If there is a lot of rain and the drains can't cope with all the water, then flooding can occur.

b Urbanization: overflowing drains can't cope with all the water

c Deforestation: cutting down large areas of trees means water can move more quickly

CHALLENGE

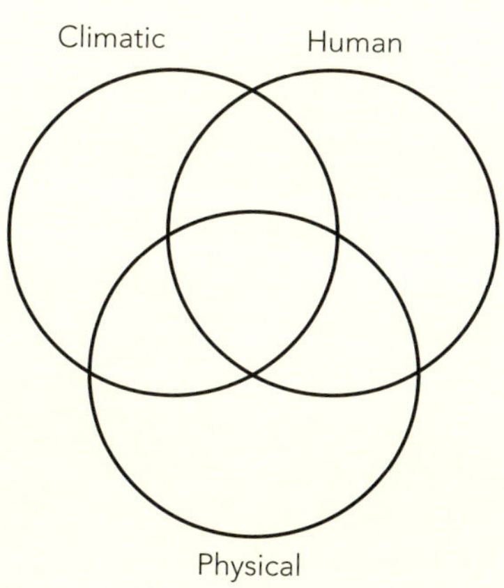

1 *Very often in geography things are easier to talk about if you can put them into categories. We can split the six main causes of flooding into three categories:*

- *Climatic – weather related causes*
- *Human – the causes that people create*
- *Physical – caused by features of the land.*

Copy the Venn diagram and add the six main causes of flooding to your diagram.

HINT: *Remember to think about which causes fit into more than one category and put them into an overlapping part of the diagram.*

d Extreme amounts of rainfall meant the ground became saturated

Why did central England flood in Summer 2007?

Rainfall in central England in June and early July was much heavier than average in 2007. Some places saw rainfall almost every day for six weeks and the ground became saturated. A lot of this rain fell on built-up areas.

Rain is often associated with low pressure systems. Think back to the water cycle:

when there is low pressure air rises → as air rises it condenses → condensation results in precipitation

On Monday 16 July, a large area of low pressure got stuck over central and western England. Map e shows this band of low pressure. It rained heavily for four days. Friday 20 July was the worst day. 150mm of rainfall was recorded officially in some areas, and amateur weather reporters recorded rainfall of up to 220mm. Rainfall was less from Saturday 21 July.

e A weather map showing low pressure across central and western England. If low pressure moves slowly and gets stuck, all the rain will fall in one place

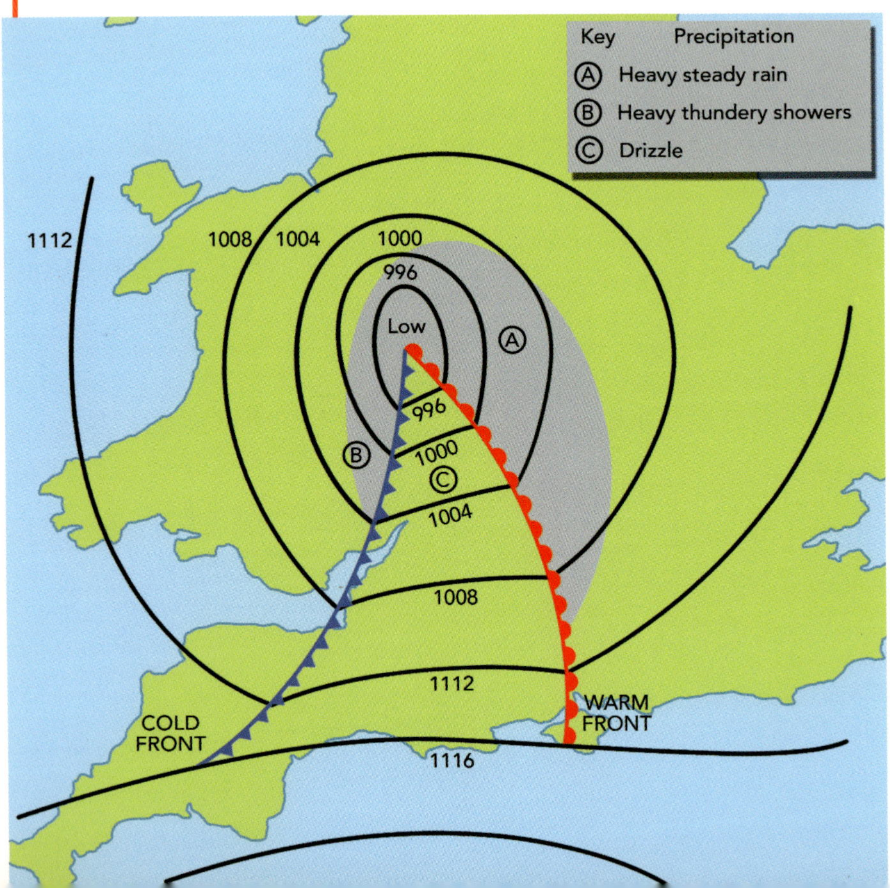

f Mobile pumping stations were sent to clear water from waterlogged roads

CHALLENGE

2 Explain, in three sentences, why central England flooded in the summer of 2007.
Think about:
a) Climatic causes
b) Human causes
c) Physical causes
Use your Venn diagram and figures d to i to help you.

The impacts of the flooding

Geographers make sense of events by judging their impact.

- Localized floods are recorded across the Midlands, centred on Evesham in Worcestershire.
- The River Avon rises to more than five metres above its normal level.
- The M5 is closed and 10 000 people spend the night stranded on the motorway.
- Holiday parks are evacuated by Air Sea Rescue helicopters.
- Bridges are closed as debris builds up and they threaten to collapse.
- Tewkesbury is worst affected as the Rivers Severn and Avon meet, creating a huge lake. Tewkesbury is completely cut off.
- Roads collapse as streams that run underneath them become swollen with water.
- Tewkesbury's water pumping station is flooded and the water supply is contaminated. 350 000 homes are without water for more than a week.
- Gloucester electricity station is within centimetres of being swamped. Emergency pumps and sandbags keep it open and power to 25 000 homes is maintained.
- The cost of the flooding was unknown at the time, but it is estimated that insurance claims will run to £1.5 billion.
- 900 water bowsers (tankers) are sent to Gloucestershire.
- The rain eases but the problem moves downstream to Abingdon and Oxford as the floodwater begins to flow down the River Thames.

g People are airlifted to safety

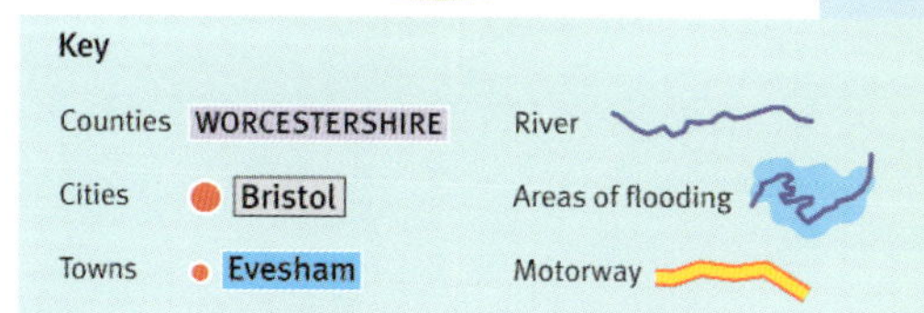

h The worst affected areas

CHALLENGE

3 Some of the impacts of the floods were more significant than others.
   a) Choose the nine most significant impacts of the summer floods of 2007.
   b) Complete a 'diamond nine' with your chosen impacts. Put the most important impact at the top, the next two most important impacts underneath and so on until you come to the least important impact at the bottom of the diamond. How are you going to choose where each impact should go? What makes an impact more or less significant? Be ready to explain your ideas.

4 There have been many floods in the UK throughout the twentieth century. What criteria could we use to decide which were the worst? **HINT:** Think about the impacts of the floods in central England in the summer of 2007.

i Residents sandbag their homes to try to keep the water out

Why are some countries wetter than others?

Some parts of the world are more likely to experience flooding than others. Using what we know about some of the causes of flooding, we will explore why this is and how these countries cope with floods.

Why do countries flood?

- Countries at or below sea level are more likely to flood because there is nowhere for the flood water to go.
- Countries with climates that often have extreme weather events – such as tropical cyclones, hurricanes and monsoons, which all bring huge amounts of rain – are more likely to flood.
- In some countries, people have tried to manage flood risk but have made it worse, making these areas more likely to flood.

Countries which are at greater risk of flooding need to take measures to manage the impacts of flooding.

We are going to look at two places in the world that have suffered serious flooding in recent years and the impact this has had.

a Bangladeshi struggle through flood water

Impacts of the floods

- 14 million people suffered.
- Over 100 people were killed.
- One million acres of crops were destroyed.
- 1000km of roads and highways were flooded.
- Many embankments that protected coastal areas from flooding were damaged.

Bangladesh, July 2007

b

In July 2007, Bangladesh, in South East Asia, experienced some of the worst flooding for several years. Some physical reasons contributed to the flooding:

- Bangladesh is very low lying, with 70% of the land area less than 1m above sea level.
- Tropical cyclones travel up the Bay of Bengal. This causes large amounts of rain to fall.
- Melting snows in the Himalayas add to water levels in the summer monsoon season.
- 80% of the country is flood plain and delta.
- Bangladesh is at the confluence of three major rivers: the River Brahmaputra, the River Meghna and the River Ganges.

Bangladesh is also a less economically developed country (LEDC), where the standard of living is low, and it is one of the most densely populated countries in the world. To feed the growing population, parts of the forested areas in Bangladesh have been cut down and turned into agricultural land. Unfortunately this deforestation makes the land even more likely to flood.

New Orleans, August 2005

In August 2005, Hurricane Katrina hit south-eastern America. One of the worst impacts of the hurricane was the flooding of New Orleans in the state of Louisiana. The flooding occurred for a mixture of human and physical reasons:

- 80% of the bowl-shaped city of New Orleans is below sea level.
- The storm surge (a surge of sea water caused by the hurricane) ripped across Lake Pontchartrain and damaged the levees (embankments) that protected New Orleans.
- Because of the damaged levees, once the water got in it was very difficult for it to drain back out again.

Impacts of the floods

- The hurricane cost America $84 billion.
- 1836 people are thought to have died, 1577 from Louisiana.
- 80% of all properties in New Orleans were damaged by water.
- Nearly one million people were without electricity for several weeks.
- One million people fled New Orleans following evacuation advice; around 80 000 stayed.

c

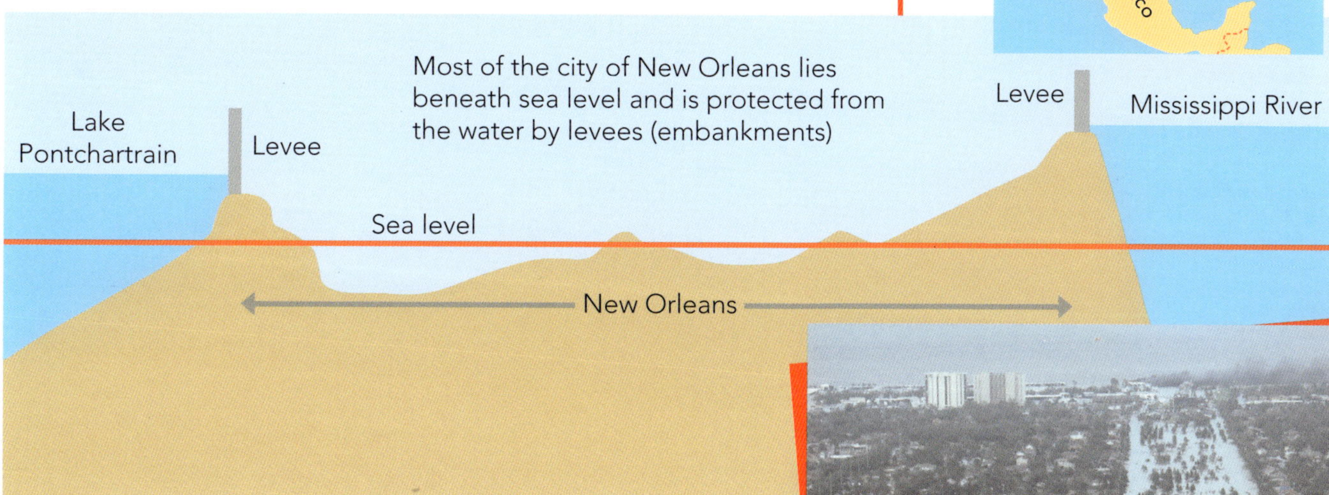

d New Orleans under water in 2005

CHALLENGE

1 Compare the flooding in Bangladesh and New Orleans. Think about:

- Where was the flooding?
- Did the flooding happen in an MEDC (a more economically developed country) or an LEDC (a less economically developed country)?
- Why did the flooding happen?
- What were the impacts of the flooding?

2 Write a short paragraph discussing which was the more serious disaster, and explaining why you made the decision you did.

What is a drought?

Just as too much water can be disastrous, too little water can also have extreme effects. Not having enough water can cause droughts and droughts have serious impacts on both LEDCs and MEDCs.

a The remains of the Haweswater reservoir in the village of Mardale Common, Cumbria which was affected by drought in 1995

CHALLENGE

1 On a blank world map, shade all the places that you think suffer from droughts.
2 In an atlas, find a world map which shows very dry (arid) areas. These areas suffer droughts.
   a) How do the dry areas match with your map?
   b) On another blank world map:
      - shade the places that do suffer from droughts.
      - label at least six countries which suffer from droughts.

What is a drought?

A drought is a continuous period of time where less precipitation falls than expected. The definition changes for different parts of the world. In the UK a drought is defined as 15 continuous days where less than 0.25mm of rain falls in any 24 hours. But some parts of the world have naturally dry climates. So in parts of Africa, for example, a drought is defined as two years or more in which there has been less than average rainfall.

What causes droughts?

Severe droughts occur when two or more of the following factors are combined.

1 **Lack of rainfall** If it doesn't rain, you expect the land to be dry.
2 **Lack of snowfall** Many places at higher altitudes rely on snowmelt from mountains for water.
3 **Ridges of high pressure** If a high pressure stays still for a long period of time, then the normal process of air rising and water vapour condensing will stop. There may be rain occurring either side of the high pressure but not under it.

If we understand weather patterns we can attempt to predict where droughts will occur.

b Animals which have died because of drought

What are the impacts of droughts?

Droughts have very serious impacts. Geographers like to put the impacts that share similar features into groups; this is called classification. Impacts of drought can be classified as direct or indirect:

- **Direct impacts** are things that happen as an inevitable consequence of not having enough water, such as crops not growing.
- **Indirect impacts** happen as a result of the direct impacts – they are the 'knock-on' effects. For example, the indirect impact of crops not growing is an increase in the price of food because it is in short supply.

Impacts can also be classified as social, environmental or economic:

- **Social impacts** affect people and their quality of life.
- **Environmental impacts** affect the habitats and ecosystems of an area.
- **Economic impacts** are things that prevent the normal economic cycle. They might stop people earning money or mean that people have to pay more for certain goods.

Some impacts fall into more than one group.

c A woman looks for water in a dried up well

d Local residents travel long distances to find water

CHALLENGE

3 Copy the circle diagram and add these impacts to the correct part of the diagram. Add any others that you can think of.

- Crops can't grow well
- Ships can't travel on waterways
- Clay soils shrink, causing structural damage to buildings
- People suffer mental and physical stress
- Endangered species are wiped out
- There is little or no fresh drinking water
- There is an increased risk of disease as food and water run short
- People move from the country to towns
- Without crops to sell, farmers struggle to earn a living
- Farmers need to spend more money on irrigation

HINT: Remember that some impacts may fit into more than one category.

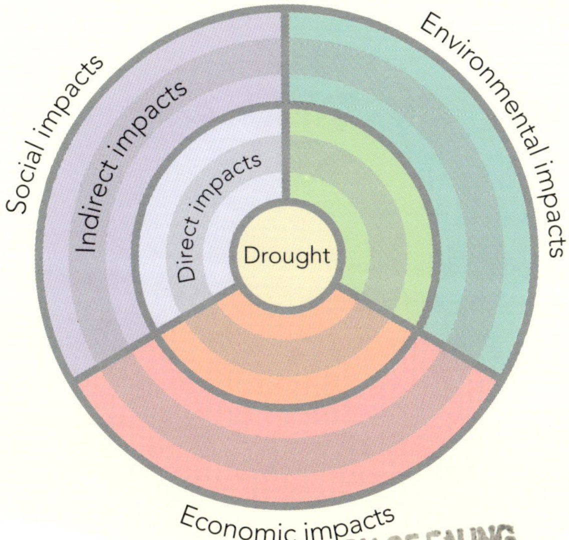

Drought in Australia, 2000–2007

FACT FILE: Australia

Population:	21 million
Area:	7.7 million km^2
Life expectancy:	78 (male) 83 (female)
Exports:	metals, wool, fuel

Australia has a varied landscape and climate. In southern Australia, the Murray–Darling drainage basin normally has a moderate climate but rainfall is erratic. The area has a mixture of scrubland, desert and farmland.

From 2000–2007 this area suffered from a drought, which Australians call the 'the big dry'. The rainfall was lower than at any time since records began in the1850s.

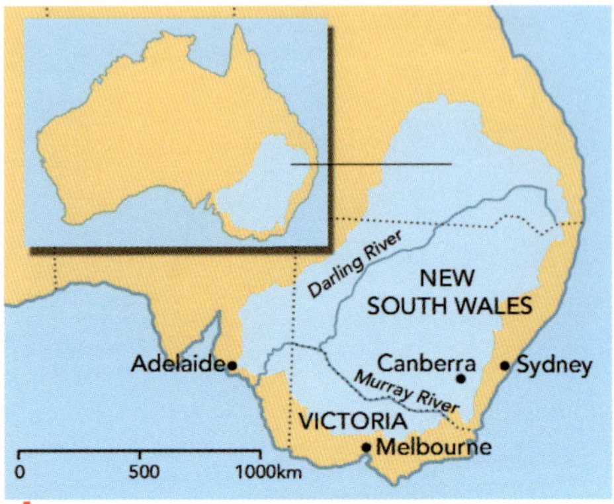

a The Murray–Darling Basin

b The Murray–Darling Basin before the drought

c The Murray–Darling Basin during the drought

CHALLENGE

4 a) Draw a circle diagram like the one on page 21 and use it to help you classify the impacts of the drought in Australia. Note that not all the sectors will be completed.

b) Add any other impacts you can think of.

Impacts of the drought:

- Crop yields are massively reduced.
- The government has to subsidise farmers to stop them going out of business. In 2007, this cost $1.7 million a day!
- Suicide rates rise because of stress and anxiety.
- Australia's total economy is reduced by 1%.
- The government has to take control of states to co-ordinate drought action.
- The koala bear's natural habitat is damaged.

Drought in Afghanistan, 1996–2007

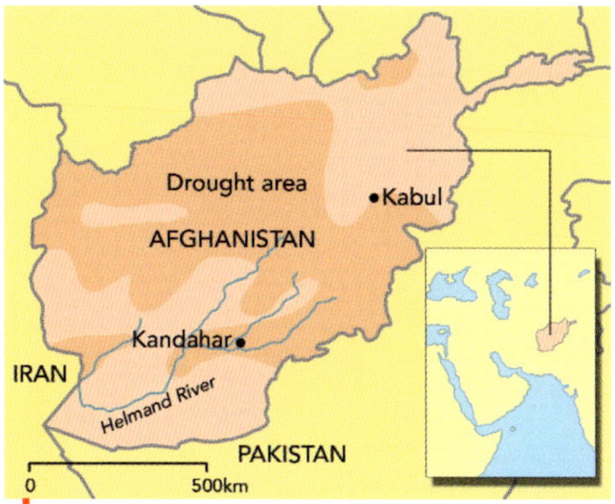

d Afghanistan

Under normal climatic conditions, Afghanistan has fertile soil irrigated by snowmelts and spring rains. The farmland produces wheat, melons, vegetables and pomegranates. However, between 1996 and 2007, Afghanistan experienced eight years that were classed as drought years due to low snowfall and rain levels.

FACT FILE: Afghanistan

Population:	26 million
Area:	652 000km^2
Life expectancy:	46 (male and female)
Exports:	fruit, nuts, carpets, wool, opium

e Afghanistan before the drought

f Afghanistan during the drought

Impacts of the drought:

- Crops fail on a large scale.
- The range of crops produced is much less than normal.
- Food prices rise by 50%.
- The poppy crop increases because it does well in drier climates. Opium, the key ingredient in heroin, is made from poppies.
- Hot sand is blown across previously farmable areas and desertification increases.
- People move to urban areas from the country.
- People suffer starvation and homelessness.

CHALLENGE

5 Draw a circle diagram and use it to help you classify the impacts of the drought in Afghanistan.

6 Look at the similarities and differences between the impacts in Australia and Afghanistan. Where do you think drought has had more impact: Australia or Afghanistan? Why?

Why are some countries drier than others?

Water is not always in plentiful supply but it is essential for our survival. In this lesson, we will discover why water is a key element in enabling a country to develop economically. We will also look at the serious effects of not having water.

Access to water around the world

a The world map shows that different areas have different levels of access to water.

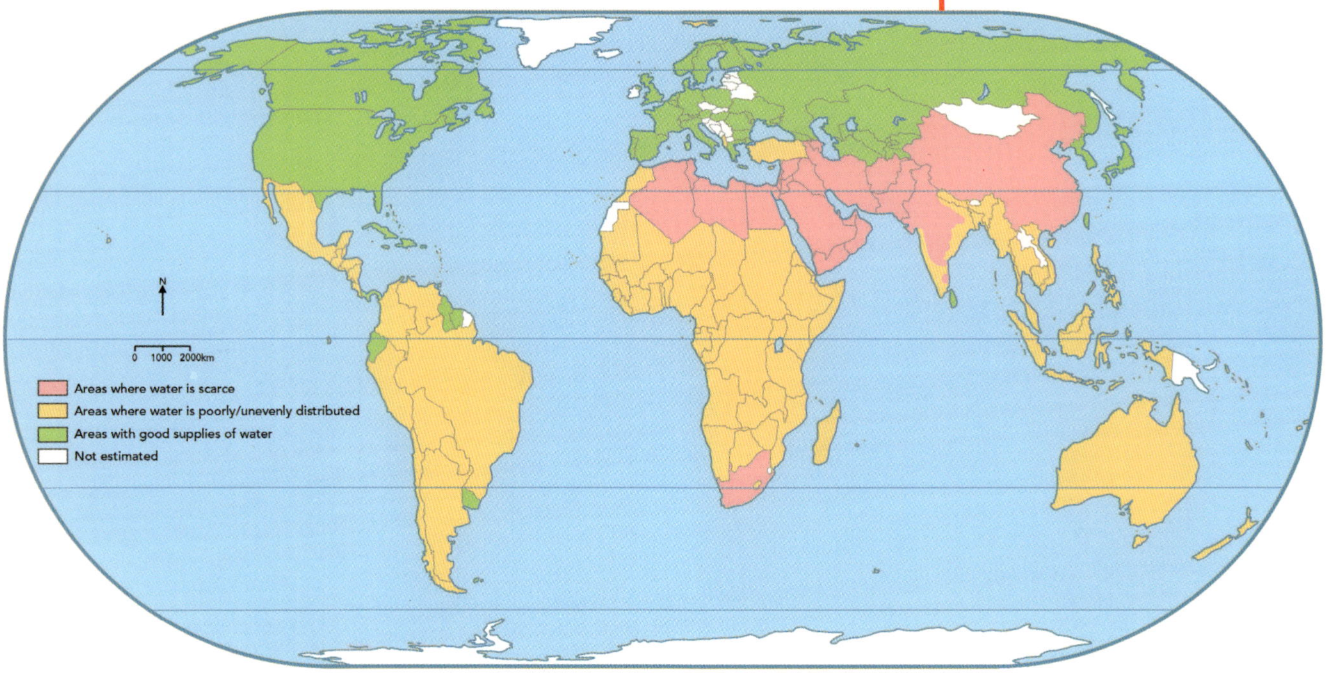

What causes different amounts of water around the world?

- **Where you are in the world** Different areas have different climates. Brazil's tropical rainforest has more than 2000mm of rain each year; northern Africa has less than 250mm.
- **How concentrated the rainfall is** In India, most of the rain falls during the monsoon season, from June to September, when heavy rainstorms can lead to flooding. The flood waters come quickly but also leave quickly, meaning the water can't be stored or used.
- **How reliable the rainfall patterns are** In some places the rainfall is unreliable: it just doesn't arrive when it's supposed to.
- **How many people live in the area** More water is needed to support growing populations. Mexico City's population grew from 15 million in 1990 to over 19 million in 2005. Parts of the city are sinking by 40cm a year because extra water has been drawn from underground rivers.
- **Climate change** Scientists know that the world's climate is changing and that this is affecting weather patterns. Places that already have unreliable rainfall could receive even less rain. Areas with a Mediterranean climate could become like deserts.

What is the link between water and economic growth?

MEDCs such as the UK would not have developed economically without water.

Everything we do revolves around water. This is because it is a basic resource and we couldn't survive without it. Below are just some of the ways that water has allowed MEDCs to develop:

- **Industrial revolution** The late eighteenth century was a time of major technological and social change, as industry developed. Many manufacturing processes needed water for cooling, and for energy.
- **Hygiene** A successful country needs a healthy workforce. Clean piped water and sanitation help to make this possible.
- **Agriculture** The climate of the UK is temperate, which means we have a balance of reliable rain and sunshine. This means we can grow a range of crops so that we don't have to spend money on importing food if we don't want to.
- **Recreation** Many pastimes such as sailing, surfing and fishing rely on water. They provide jobs and the money made from them can be ploughed back into the economy.
- **Energy** Increasingly, water is becoming more important as a renewable energy source, through methods such as hydro-electric power and tidal power. In the past, water wheels generated energy.

b How much water do you use every day?

c How many of your pastimes involve water?

CHALLENGE

1 There are many other ways in which water has helped MEDCs to develop. How many can you think of? Try to think of groups that you could use to classify them.

What are the impacts of a lack of water on LEDCs?

The map on page 24 shows that many of the places with poor access to water are LEDCs in the developing world. How does that affect their development?

- **Health** Dirty water causes 80% of diseases in developing countries. These diseases include cholera, typhoid, diarrhoea and dysentery. Children are especially at risk.
- **Education** Many LEDCs have no access to piped water, children are sent to collect it. Collecting water is physically stressful and very time consuming and, as a result, girls are often too busy to attend school.
- **Agriculture** Lack of water makes it difficult for plants to grow and animals to stay healthy and productive. Without water, crops fail, animals die and people suffer from malnutrition.
- **Family life** Because children have to collect water, they have little time to enjoy family life and have to grow up very quickly.
- **Social unrest** People may fight over the few water resources available, leading to social problems.

When you add all of these effects together they have a very big impact on how a country can develop.

As long as the levels of development remain low, the quality of life will remain poor – all because of a lack of water.

d Women washing clothes in a river in Mgeta District in Tanzania

CHALLENGE

2 Imagine that you live in an LEDC. You are appalled at how people in MEDCs waste and pollute their water supplies. Write a speech to explain to people in MEDCs how lucky they are and why they should use their water supplies more carefully.
HINT: Remember to use as many different pieces of geographical evidence as possible.

e Slum dwellers scramble for water in Kusumpur Pahari, Delhi, India

Why do we need to use water more sustainably?

The water cycle shows that there is only so much water on the planet. But the world population is growing. It will reach over nine billion by 2045. And all these people need water. Without it, a person can live for only ten days!

How much water do we use?

In MEDCs, each person uses about 153 litres of water a day. In LEDCs, each person uses less than 25 litres. So how do MEDCs manage to use so much water? Even the most basic activities use large amounts of water:

- Brushing teeth with the tap running – 1 litre
- Having a bath – 80 litres
- Flushing the toilet – 8 litres
- Having a shower – 35 litres
- Using the washing machine – 65 litres
- Using the dishwasher – 25 litres

So by using a dishwasher once we are using the same amount of water that a person in the developing world has to live on for an entire day!

It's not just how much we use; it's also what we're doing to the quality of the water. Human activities such as farming, industry and transport are spoiling the quality of water by polluting it with insecticides, fertilisers and industrial waste.

If you use something sustainably it means that you are using it now while making sure that there is enough for future generations. The amount of water we are using, wasting and polluting is going to make life for future generations difficult, so it is clearly not sustainable. What can we do to improve things?

We can all make a difference. Try some of these:

- Turn off the tap when you're brushing your teeth.
- Wash the car with a bucket, not a hosepipe.
- Get a waterbutt to collect rain-water and use it to water the garden.
- Only flush the toilet when you really need to.

f

g

CHALLENGE

3 There is a limited amount of water in the water cycle. With people using so much water and a rapidly rising world population, will we have enough water in the future? Come up with an action plan of what we could do to improve the situation. Your action plan should include:

- the reasons why we need to reduce the amount of water we use
- the main factors that have led to people using so much water
- the actions we can take to use water more carefully.

What are NGOs and what do they do?

As responsible global citizens we should know what we can do to help people who don't have access to enough water. One of the ways in which we can help is to support Non-Governmental Organisations (NGOs). In this lesson we will find out about one of these: WaterAid.

WaterAid charity reg no 288701

What is an NGO?

An NGO is a voluntary group that works at a local, national or international level, but not for profit. NGOs are involved with a range of issues, from human rights to the environment and health. The International Red Cross, Greenpeace, Oxfam, Amnesty International and Doctors without Borders (Médecins Sans Frontières) are all NGOs, as is WaterAid, an NGO that deals specifically with water.

What is WaterAid?

WaterAid is an international charity. Its mission is to overcome poverty by helping the world's poorest people gain access to safe water, sanitation and hygiene education. These basic human rights underpin health, education and livelihoods. They are the essential first steps in overcoming poverty.

Working with people and organisations already in the country, WaterAid supports communities by helping them to gain the skills to set up and manage their own sustainable projects. This will help them to meet their real water needs.

The technology used by WaterAid is always low-cost and appropriate to the locations. It depends on the community's needs and water sources in the area. Knowledge of weather patterns is also a vital part of finding solutions. For example, countries which experience low amounts of rainfall during certain times of the year may not find rainwater harvesting useful. Two different methods are:

- **Rainwater harvesting** Falling rainwater is some of the cleanest water available. Water is collected from pre-cleaned rooftops where it runs, via guttering, into a storage tank.
- **Hand-dug wells** Hand-dug wells are the most common method of extracting water in LEDCs. WaterAid helps communities to develop wells that can quickly become the centre of village life.

a A hand-dug well

WaterAid in Ethiopia

Ethiopia is in East Africa and although it is has a rich history it is best known for the droughts it experienced in the 1980s. Today, Ethiopia still faces serious problems:

- Only 22% of the population have access to safe water.
- Only 6% of the population have adequate sanitation.

WaterAid has been supporting projects in Ethiopia since 1983. These have included building toilets for houses and organisations, hygiene education, especially hand washing, and involving women and minority groups in helping with future projects. By 2010 it aims to help 100 000 people gain access to water and 95 000 gain access to sanitation and hygiene education every year.

FACT FILE: Ethiopia

Population:	71 million
Area:	1 128 000km^2
Life expectancy:	47 (male and female)

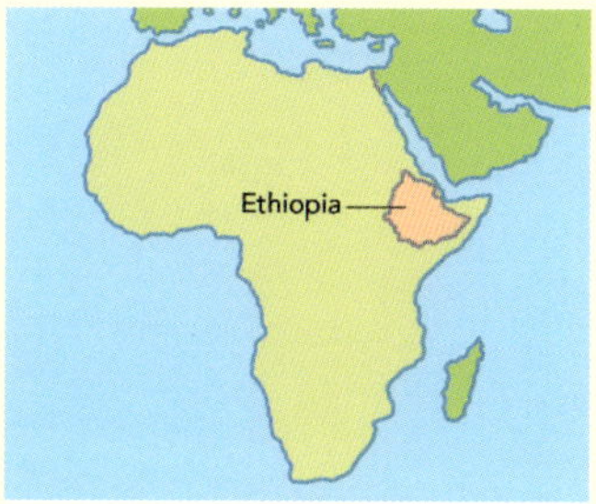

b A WaterAid worker explains how to practice hygiene safely

How can campaigns make a difference?

WaterAid role uses geographical knowledge to determine how best to use technology in LEDCs. It is also important for WaterAid to work in the UK to raise awareness of its work through the media, in order to raise money.

A WaterAid campaign officer's main responsibilities are to communicate with and support those who wish to take action on behalf of the organisation. A campaign officer has to stay informed about the latest policy on water and sanitation in the developing world.

CHALLENGE

1 Imagine that you are a campaign officer for WaterAid. Design a leaflet to communicate the issues about water and developing countries. Include the following information:

- why access to clean water is important for development
- what WaterAid can do to help change things
- a case study, including maps, diagrams, graphs and photos.

More information about WaterAid can be found at www.wateraid.org/uk.

HINT: Use as many different sources as possible.

Glossary

Abrasion The erosion process by which river load wears away the bed and banks like sandpaper

Attrition The erosion process by which material carried in the river collides causing pieces of the material to be chipped off

Campaign officer A person who believes in and alerts other people to important causes

Condensation The process by which water vapour becomes a liquid when cooled

Confluence The location where two rivers meet

Deforestation The cutting down of forested areas for agriculture, industry or homebuilding

Delta The landform created by the deposition of sediment where a river meets the sea

Deposition The process by which material is dropped by moving water, usually because of a fall in energy levels

Desertification The process by which desert landscapes are extended to a larger area because of drought conditions and climate change

Development The process of improving a country and its standard of living

Drainage basin The area of land around a river which drains into it

Drought A continuous period of time where little precipitation falls in comparison with what is expected

Erosion The process by which worn material is removed by an agent such as ice, water or wind

Evaporation The process by which liquid water which has been heated turns into water vapour

Flooding The over-spilling of water when there is too much to be contained within the normal channel

Gorge A steep-sided river valley

Groundwater flow The movement of groundwater towards the river channel

Hydraulic action The erosion process by which fast-flowing water in rivers forces air in gaps in the river bank to become compressed and act like mini-explosions

Interlocking spurs The landform created by a river following the V-shaped valley in the upper course of a river – like a giant zip

LEDC Less economically developed country – a country where the standard of development and quality of living are low

Levee The humped looking landforms formed either side of a river by flooding events. These can also be a man-made river management technique

Long profile The cross-section of a river's gradient from the mouth to the source

Lower course The generally flat lower section of the river

Meander A bend in a river

MEDC More economically developed country – a country where the standard of development and quality of living are high

Middle course The middle section of a river

Mouth The end of a river where it flows into the sea

NGO Non-Governmental Organisation

Overland flow The movement of water across a surface due to heavy rainfall or saturated ground

Oxbow lake The lake formed when the neck of the meander becomes so small it is cut through

Plunge pool A deep pool created by the erosion from a waterfall

Precipitation Any form of moisture in the atmosphere falling to earth – hail, rain, sleet, snow

River bank The sides of the river

River bed The bottom of the river channel

River channel The trough shape which the river flows through

Saltation The transport process by which pebble-sized particles leapfrog over each other

Sea level The average level of the surface of the sea

Solution The process by which certain chemicals are dissolved out of the bed, banks and load of rivers. This can be both a form of erosion and transportation

Source The area high in the mountains where a river starts

Storm surge A rise in offshore water associated with hurricanes and tropical storms caused by winds pushing on the ocean surface

Suspension The transport method by which very small particles are carried along in the river's flow

Sustainable Able to meet our current living and resource needs without spoiling the ability of future generations to meet theirs. Sustainability means using resources sensibly

Through flow Water in the soil which moves sideways through the spaces (pores)

Traction The transport process by which large boulders at the start of the river are rolled along the river bed irregularly

Transpiration The process by which liquid water is breathed out as water vapour by plants

Transportation The process by which river load is moved from one area of a river to another

Tributary A small river which joins a larger river

Upper course The upper section of a river

Urbanization The process by which locations become more city like

V-shaped valley The steep-sided valley shape seen in the upper course of a river

Water cycle The continuous cycle of water on a global scale which involves evaporation, condensation, precipitation and transpiration

Water table The boundary between the underground rock spaces which are saturated with water and rock spaces which are not

Waterfall The landform made when a river flows over a steep drop

Watershed The imaginary line around a drainage basin

Index